W9-ACX-030

MUSIC AND WOMEN

From *Jahreshefte des Oesterreichischen
Archaologischen Inst. vol. 12-13, 1909-10*

Frontispiece. A *Hekateion* unites the spirits of the
waxing, full, and waning moon: Artemis, Selene,
and Hekate. In this lovely ivory figurine from ancient Greece, dancing maidens invoke the three-fold
goddess to keep them in the flow of all life.

(See page 122.)

MUSIC
AND WOMEN

THE STORY OF WOMEN IN THEIR
RELATION TO MUSIC

BY
SOPHIE DRINKER

ZENGER

PUBLISHING CO. INC.

BOX 31061 • WASHINGTON DC 20031

COPYRIGHT, 1948, BY SOPHIE DRINKER.

All rights reserved. This book, or parts thereof, must not be reproduced in any form without permission.

Published simultaneously in the Dominion of Canada by Longmans, Green & Company, Toronto.

MANUFACTURED IN THE UNITED STATES OF AMERICA.

✓ ML
82
.D7
1977

Reprinted
With Permission
1977

Library of Congress Cataloging in Publication Data

Drinker, Sophie Lewis Hutchinson.
   Music and women.

   Reprint of the ed. published by Coward–McCann, New York.
   Includes bibliographical references.
   1. Women musicians.   I.   Title.
ML82.D7   1977   780'.07   75–35730
ISBN 0–89201–011–8

CONTENTS

ILLUSTRATIONS

FOREWORD

MY ORIGINAL incentive to write a book about women in their relation to music came from a women's chorus that met for fifteen years in the music room of my home. It was my responsibility to find appropriate music for my friends who gathered here to sing—women like myself, neighbors with husband, children, and home.

From the beginning I was both surprised and shocked at the type of choral literature offered by the music publishers. It was childish, trivial, far too sentimental for these intelligent women who took time out of their busy lives for spiritual exaltation. It was, indeed, listed in many catalogues as music intended for "women's and *children's* voices"! I was amazed that the modern woman, with her high education, her personal liberty, and her active participation in the life of the community, was satisfied to sing, in a group, music manifestly inferior to other works of the same composers for solo voice or mixed chorus.

Almost none of the music we sang was composed by women. Why, I wondered, do my contemporaries, with their aspiration to self-expression, their notable attainments in this direction, neither excel as individual creators of the important music of our civilization nor even use a natural musical ability as a common mode of self-expression? Women musicians are experts in performing vocal and instrumental music, but rarely do they play or sing music that they themselves have composed. Why do they allow themselves to be merely carriers of the creative musical imagination of men? Why do they not use the language of music, as they use gesture and speech, to communicate their own ideas and feelings?

It is not necessary here to emphasize the value of music in relation to spiritual stature. Philosophers of all ages have dwelt upon the importance of music as both an outlet for the spirit and emotions and as discipline for the mind. It is generally recognized that music gives access to regions in the subconscious that can be reached in no other way. By plumbing depths where nature and spirit are in unity, a greater awareness of surrounding conditions may be developed and other inherent native talents may be stimulated into activity. Women's failure to think in terms of their own creative music has the inevitable result of causing a kind of feminine spiritual starvation. Moreover, it thins the quality of musical feeling and expression in general.

My intense interest in the enrichment of women's inner lives led me, therefore, from document to document, from book to book and article to article, from interview to interview with musicologists and specialists in other forms of learning related to this one, in my search for an understanding of women and music.

Among the countless things I wanted and needed to know were these, as illustrative: Had anyone undertaken a methodical analysis of early women's dirges and offered explanations for their composition? Did Victoria create his beautiful women's chorus "Duo Seraphim" for the Empress Maria and the nuns of Descalzas Reales in Madrid? Did ladies in medieval castles merely repeat songs improvised by men for their entertainment or did they evolve songs of their own? In modern times did American women play instruments with men in such musical groups as the Boston Flute Players Club? Where could I get the answers?

Grove's Dictionary of Music and Musicians was more of a puzzle than a source of information for my purposes. General histories of music rarely mention women. Wider histories of a general nature commonly ignore music while dealing with the "people." Fully half of the authors to whom I turned for knowledge, since they took account of women in connection with music, affirmed the passivity of women in this art except as inspirers of masculine musicians. Even in a book on *Woman in Music* carrying chapters headed Bach, Beethoven, Schubert, and Schumann, I discovered that women were depicted only as friends or relatives of these famous men musicians.

Yet I refused to be completely discouraged; I was firmly convinced that the whole story of music had not been told in a single volume, in any compendium of information on music, or in any collected series of works on the subject. I determined to find woman in this larger story of musical creativeness where I believed she belonged.

As I proceeded to read and to make independent inquiries, I did in fact find a great mass of material, both written and pictorial, concerning women and music. There were the rock paintings revealing women musicians. There were myths and legends about the musical activities of hundreds of goddesses and other feminine spirits—symbols and reflections of women in real life. There were the songs and dances of primitive women and of peasants. There were many references in scattered sources to Egyptian, Sumerian, Cretan, Greek, Roman, Chinese, East Indian, Arabian, and Jewish women musicians and also to the famous Saracen singing girls with their descendants at the court of the Great Mogul. There was proof of the participation of Christian women in the music of the early organized groups of Christ's followers. There were descriptions of women musicians from medieval times to the modern age. There were also musical scores demonstrating the character of a considerable amount of women's compositions.

From books in which this factual material appeared I have assembled, classified, and arranged pertinent items in manageable form. With my complete bibliography they may be studied in the Smith College and in the University of Pennsylvania libraries. The material on goddesses has been segregated for an article requested by the *Encyclopaedia Britannica* and will appear there in a forthcoming edition. It is my intention ultimately to make a reference book dealing exclusively with women's symbols and deities. Since pictures are indispensable in a comprehensive history of women and music, illustrations accompany each folio of collected material. Reinforcing the power of the written word, they positively portray musicians and they demonstrate the connection of women musicians with religious rites such as goddess worship and with the personal exuberance of women's spirit.

My distillation of facts for the present volume begins with four chapters on women as musicians in living groups of people called primitives and peasants. Why do I start with women of these types? There are two reasons: one is that the musical activities of such women, as in all modern researches for social origins, suggest the forms that prehistoric musical vitality assumed; the other is the clear evidence that such women are customarily on footings of equality or superiority with men in the realm of musical invention. In conformity with the practices of modern anthropological work, therefore, as well as with the findings that indicate a natural musicianship among women, the background of woman's musicianship in history is first brought to attention.

No doubt it is obvious that this volume is useful as an assortment of information about women's historic musical activities, but its true value would be missed if it were viewed merely in that way. Simply to cull items from it, as one might from a catalogue of musical events or descriptions, would be to tear apart things inseparably related; such as the intimacy between women's musicianship, their emotional reactions to productive labor, and their conceptions of the whole spiritual aspect of life, including their associations with men and children. Great music has always been rooted in religion—when religion is understood as an *attitude* toward superhuman power and the mysteries of the universe. This sensitivity to life, to its aims, its commands, its forms, and to its supporting emotions within men and women is a phase of the feminine being that, if deeply understood, should operate as an incitement to musicians, artists, poets, dancers, and all persons who long for a greater art expression in our modern world.

It is now nearly twenty years since I began to collect facts and to formulate ideas about women in their relation to music. During this long time, certain people have encouraged me beyond the point of polite interest in a neglected subject. Fundamentally, their support consisted in an understanding of my long and hard study in preparation for handling so difficult a matter, coupled with faith that the kind of book I had in mind could illuminate women's aptitude for musical composition, and induce in that light an impulse to more creativeness. From the beginning, the steadfast encouragement of my husband has been my greatest boon. His respect for me as an individual, creative in my own right, gave me the spiritual sustenance required for the expression of any original thinking.

For continuously challenging the validity of my interpretations and helping me to verify them from the authority of their own experience and knowledge, several women have my sincere gratitude. In that respect, Harriet Gratwick, Mabel Carnarius, Lela Vauclain, and my daughters live in these pages. In the early days when my project was in its infancy, Kathi Meyer, at that time librarian of the Paul Hirsch Library at Frankfurt am Main, opened the door to fruitful lines of research. Her wide musicological knowledge, so freely shared, has been a benefaction to me ever since. Katherine Swan, Russian sociologist and philologist, wrote for me an account of the participation of Russian women of all classes in music. Louise Beck, collaborator with Jean Beck in his work on the troubadours of France, gave me details about the musical activities of medieval ladies. Ruth Benedict, in the Department of Anthropology at Columbia University, taught me that woman's musical imagination depends upon the culture pattern of any given group for development as definitely as does any other human characteristic. The first to give me systematic editorial help was Katherine R. Drinker, at one time managing editor of the *Journal of Industrial Hygiene*. From first to last, Ann Chase has been constructively reviewing versions of the manuscript from the point of view of philosophy and psychology, and Catherine Drinker Bowen has as continuously given me the benefit of her great skill in the use of English. Mary R. Beard, who has written on women in long history but exclusive of the woman musician, warmly and generously reassured me that my efforts to introduce this feature of women's capability were socially important.

When I discovered that primitive women often displayed remarkable evidence of creative imagination, Heinrich A. Wieschhoff, curator of the African section of the University of Pennsylvania Museum, patiently answered a myriad of questions about rock paintings and primitive customs. More recently, M. F. Ashley-Montagu, associate professor of anatomy at Hahnemann Hospital in Philadelphia, checked my social anthropological data, and William Schuman, director of the Juilliard School of Music, approved the section on modern developments for the woman musician. The efficiency of Arthur Hamlin, assistant librarian in the service division of the University of Pennsylvania Library, in locating obscure books and articles has been a constant spur to continued research.

To Marjorie Barstow Greenbie I am indebted for final editorial services, which words cannot measure. Her long literary experience, coupled with Sydney Greenbie's wise advice, helped me to keep excessive details within bounds, to explain certain passages that might otherwise have been obscure to the general reader, to highlight several matters that I had perhaps underlighted, to add vivid touches from far-off places, and generally to give me confidence that my history of women in music would find popular appreciation.

I present my message, therefore, in the hope that it will remind every woman—and especially my own little granddaughters, Sophie, Ann, Ernesta, and Caroline—that they have deep, and as yet in our world, untapped reservoirs of imaginative power.

SOPHIE DRINKER

Merion, Pennsylvania
June, 1947

FULL MOON

CHAPTER I

SINGERS OF MAGIC

1.

WHEN the men of New Guinea are away at war, or on a long journey, their women beat upon booming gongs and sing to hasten the coming of the new moon. The first one to see the thin golden crescent in the sky gives a shout and all the women rejoice: "Now we see the moon, and so do our husbands, and now we know that they are well; if we do not sing, they would be sick or some other misfortune would befall them." [1]

No man composed the music. No man stands in the jungle shadows and waves his baton. No audience listens. But as the night silence deepens, and two or three tiny pinpricks of light in the village of thatched huts go out, and the young moon rides high in the sky, the voice of the leader soars as if it would lay hold of the very horns of the moon, and the voices of the others come in, rich and strong, supported by the rolling beat of the drums. The moonlight on their dark eyes and gleaming dark faces lights them into a deadly earnestness. They are not doing this to entertain anybody, even themselves. This is woman's music made by women only, for a woman's purpose. (See Plate 1.)

"If we do not sing our men will die." Theirs is an incantation or singing to invoke the powers that govern the rhythm of life. This moon that appears in the sky like a newborn baby will wax in the following nights like a growing child into a full round being. The women have power to invoke it with singing for the protection of their men, because they are the Daughters of the Moon.

Everywhere in the world simple, unlettered women who live more under the open sky than under roofs, without men's books, without men's churches and universities, feel their being as women peculiarly

3

linked to the celestial being of the moon. For the rhythmic drama of a woman's bodily life, of which childbirth is the great climax, is timed to the cycle of the moon. Her monthly cycle is four weeks or a lunar month. She measures the time it will take her to bring her child to birth by the waxing and waning of the moon. Ten times the thin, gleaming crescent will appear in the sky, ten times it will grow to its full, round, lusty prime, and ten times it will fade and shrink and so grow old and die. Ten times it will be born again. And at the tenth moon the child will be born, and grow like the moon to full splendor, and wane, and die—to be reborn again like the moon, if a woman has faith and makes the proper incantations or singing.

2.

Music in its elemental and primitive form, as still practiced by people of the simpler societies all over the world, is incantation. Incantation from Latin *cantare*, to sing, and *in*, meaning into, is literally a singing into. The primitive musician believes that by directing the force of rhythm and sound upon a thing, a person, or a situation, he can make it conform to his will.

To any honest and simple mind looking out on the wild world of living things, life is identical with rhythm and sound. A dead thing does not make a sound. Its heart does not beat. Therefore life is rhythm and sound. What is more reasonable than the application of rhythm and sound to objects, forcing into them the kind of life one wants them to have?

A Zuñi Indian woman making pottery, for instance, will imitate with her voice the sound of water boiling. This is to make the pot firm and unbreakable when water boils in it. Bavenda women pounding grain imitate the sound made by their pestles—*gu, gu*—in the mortars. Zuñi priestesses sing to the Spirit of Rain: "Fall upon the mountains and on the plains!"[2] As they pronounce the command they drop their voices in a descending scale to imitate the falling rain. Lithuanian women imitate the sounds of words that are themselves suggestive of the rustling of winds, the gurgling of water, and he trilling of birds.

In this primitive world there is rarely poetry without melody. Poems are usually sung. When asked whether words or melody came first into an artist's mind, a Hopi Indian said that song meant words and music conceived simultaneously. Where texts of songs have been written down by some visitor or literate scribe, an accompanying melody can therefore be assumed.

But this music has a practical aim. It is designed to do something. When a girl in Palestine thinking of her distant lover sings:

> "O trees, bend down to shade him,
> O stars, shine brightly for him!" [3]

she is making use of words to control the elements. And when a Greek nurse sings to a wakeful child:

> "The sun is sleeping in the mountains,
> the partridge in the woods—" [4]

her aim is to induce sleep by the power of suggestion inherent in the words. With us such words are merely poetic parlance. But these women believe them to be a practical method of attaining their ends.

As if to make their texts irresistible, women often end their formulas with words like these:

> My words, be strong and sticky, harder than stone,
> Stickier than glue or sulphur, saltier than salt,
> Sharper than a sword, stronger than steel. [5]

Out of the determination to make the words stick grows the musician's artistry. Rhythmical sounds and a variety of imitative tones reinforce the meaning of words and persuade or compel the listener to attend to them. So also do instruments. Women often make rattles by using gourds or by sewing little bags of dried skin and filling them with seeds or pebbles. They make pipes or flutes or stamping tubes by using hollow reeds or bamboo. They make the gourd zithers and probably the musical bow that in Rhodesia has nothing to do with the hunter's bow and is never used by men. Among European peasants women often use harp, dulcimer, and castanets; the tambourine is everywhere their special instrument. In many parts of the primitive world women not only use drums but make the drums themselves.

Except for drums, however, instruments are undeveloped in comparison to ours and exist generally for the purpose of making a noise to frighten away or to attract spirits. The voice is the instrument,

and vocal music has attained in many primitive cultures a high state
of artistic expression.

Just as it is obvious to the intelligent nature worshiper that life is
rhythm and sound, and that if one directs the right rhythm and
sound upon something, one puts life into it, so it is equally obvious
that women are the proper persons to make incantations. Clearly
women are more closely related to the life force than men, because
they have the power to make new human beings in their own bodies.

Moreover, in some mysterious way this power in women to make
people is related to the waxing and waning of the moon. Here, in the
sky, waxing and waning, dying and coming to life again, is the mag-
ical prototype of life. And women, who make human beings, are ob-
viously related to the moon in some special way.

So the woman's natural authority is the authority over life and
death. By singing, she who understands human birth has the power
to bring about birth everywhere. So woman's music is made in the
stupendous faith that if it is only made in the right way, it can turn
the old into new and bring the dead to life. There is thus concen-
trated in the single indivisible magic of a woman's incantation the
foundation of the modern professions of religion, medicine, and
music.

3.

I heard it while traveling—
The woman's song being sung.[6]

From the edge of the frozen tundra in the day-long night of the arctic
winter, in Canada and Siberia, to the coral reefs of the Pacific and the
green slopes of South Sea islands, which are like mountain peaks half
sunk in the sea; from the vast hot spaces of Africa to old villages
under the spruce and pine in Finland and Russia; from the foggy
Aleutian Islands to Indian pueblos, under the blazing sky of New
Mexico; in a thousand villages tucked quietly behind the peaks of
the Andes, or forgotten on the slopes of Mount Olympus; in the val-
leys of the Himalayas and by the springs of the Yangtze and the Yel-
low rivers, or lost in the folds and crannies of Central Europe—
brides, mothers, and old wives are making their own music. Blue-
eyed or dark-eyed, pink-cheeked, olive-skinned, deeply brunette;
Estonian women with smooth blonde sheets of hair; Indian women
with dark braids; African women with tight curls, each oiled and

carefully set; dark-skinned Melanesian women with bleached, bushy hair that is like a gold cap atop a vivid dark face—they are singing their incantations, their songs of joy and songs of sorrow. Through their compositions, in which words and music are of one inspiration, there resounds the story of birth, love, work, death, and rebirth, the story of hearth and home, the liturgy of woman's religion.

The primitive woman's authority over life and death, thus expressed in music, is supported by all the circumstances of primitive society.

Bringing life, fostering it with food and warmth, keeping humanity in touch with the spirit world are her normal activities. Her inborn talents all have a high value for the type of society in which she lives. What she does economically brings health and wealth to her people; what she does spiritually gives them contact with the life force. The more she asserts herself and the more she emphasizes her natural ways, the more power she brings to her tribe and the more she develops her own physical, mental, and spiritual stature. Childbearing, far from interfering, actually stimulates the development of creative imagination, especially her musical faculty. For around the physical nourishment and the spiritual aids that the mother must provide for the child, primitive family and social life are organized.

"In olden times, men and women were like two distinct peoples," [7] a Natchez Indian told an eighteenth-century French missionary. The primitive family is a considerable community of women and girls and boys under twelve, to which any number of men are more or less loosely attached. It is closely knit and self-sufficient, sustained by the women's monopoly of basic industry—the production of food and clothing. Women in primitive societies need no by-your-leave from their menfolk. They go about their business, not much caring what the men do, sure that when the time comes men will be drawn back to them by the irresistible double lure of sex and food.

Since primitive industries are centered in the communal household, the women must be well organized. There is the head of the group, usually the old mother or mother-in-law, who lectures the younger ones perpetually. She really doesn't know how she gets anything done with a lot of addlepated girls who are always planning to steal away and meet their lovers under the palm tree or the bamboo tree or the fir tree. She is annoyed with young women who are always mooning over their husbands or worrying about the babies. And she thinks the younger generation has no religion and never will learn to carry a tune or rotate their hips or shake their heels smoothly and rapidly in the community dance. Among the Maoris, where the grand old woman, work boss, priestess, and musician in one, functions at her best, she keeps after the girls from morning till night about their voices and the use of their bodies, while instructing them at intervals in all the other mysteries of life, and boring them to death with the recital of long genealogies. Thus, somehow or other, the new generation of women leaders and musicians is trained.

Subordinate to the old woman leader, but co-operating with her, are other older women, aunts, cousins, and females adopted into the household years before, down to the elder sister who is complete manager of the younger ones and responsible for all their sins.

Often women are organized into religious associations, or secret societies, by which they assert and emphasize their independence and solidarity. In certain African tribes today, women force men to remain in their huts during the performance of the secret rites. Men are convinced that their own vital powers would shrink up forever should they attempt to glance at the women's mysteries. In sex solidarity, women share their normal experiences, work in groups, play games together, help each other in childbirth, and worship their own spirits. Sometimes they speak in different language terms from those of the men. Wherever they dance, they use steps of their own invention, beat drums with their own rhythms, and sing songs of their own creation. (See Plate 2.)

Such institutions tend to develop women leaders whose authority often extends into the larger life of the community. As queen, chieftainess, priestess, prophetess, seeress, oracle, shamaness, magician, musician, and even as old wife who has experienced life, woman exercises a natural control over the members of her society. If and when women celebrate jointly with men at religious ceremonies and games, they perform as an independent unit with their own leaders.

Leadership in the fields where women have natural authority—in music, healing, and ritual—is strengthened by the attitude of the community. Among many simple people woman is highly valued for her natural bond with the life force. She is often regarded as the symbol of life itself. As long as the deep stream of mothers and daughters, bearing husbands and sons in its powerful current, flows on undisturbed, the spirit of the tribe prospers. Mothers symbolically pass the torch of life to their daughters; a girl in the bloom of youth with a moon tattooed on her back, a star on her forehead, and a turtle on her hands must dance to stimulate fertility in field and home. A May queen and a chosen youth must exchange the kiss that awakens life. Without the woman in action, there is no life *and the spirit lies dormant.* Woman's authority rests not only in birth but in the function of nourishing. Mothers are expected to feed their babies at the breast and then to provide other food. So women often identify themselves with the earth, or with grain, or with flowers and fruit. Some of the North American Indians call the corn "old woman who never dies" —the same name they have for the moon. Iroquois women regard the food spirits as their sisters and thank them with song:

> On the planted fields I walked:
> Throughout the fields I went:
> Fair fields of corn I saw there: . . . .
> I have thanked the sustainers of life.[8]

In one of the most beautiful liturgies in existence the Zuñi Indians glorify the nurturing mother. The Maiden-Mothers of the North, West, South, and East carry trays of seeds, each her own kind, as the wonderful truth is chanted:

"Lo, as a mother of her own being and blood gives life and sustenance to her offspring, so have these given unto ye—for ye are their children—the means of life and sustenance. . . . Behold! beautiful and perfect were the maidens, and as this their flesh, derived from them in beauty and by beautiful custom is perfect and beautiful, so shall it confer on those nourished of it, perfection of person and beauty. . . ."[9]

By reason of women's function as the source of food and drink for the newborn child, women are called upon to ensure, by charms and incantations, the water and the food for the community. They have authority over springs and wells, and often are the official rain charmers, passing on their magic powers to a daughter. Some peoples believe that woman's magic touch makes the grain grow. Among European peasants, where the formal ceremonies of the church have not completely superseded women's rites, women clap hands, shout, dance, shake tambourines, play pipes, and sing to celebrate the first day after midwinter and help call the spring and the season of new growth. (See Plate 3.) In Russia when spring is in the air and the birds are expected again, women bake buns in the shape of larks. Their daughters carry the buns out into the fields and call on Láda, goddess of fertility, love, and marriage.

"Bless, Mother, oi! Mother Láda!
Bless us to call the spring,
To see off the winter." [10]

Many expect a priestess rather than a priest, or priestess and priest together, to serve in the religious ceremonies organized for the purpose of praying for prosperity. Great festivals are held at regular intervals and celebrated by men and women together for the purpose of inducing fertility, of renewing the warmth of the sun, of reviving the moon, of giving thanks for harvest, of casting out evil spirits, and of propitiating the nature deities. In some places, women and men beat the drums together and have dances in which both sexes perform. Among the Hootka Indians (U.S.A.) there are mixed choruses in which the men and the women sing in harmony. In other places women have their own dances and their own magic music. The women's choir, with its own leader, brings its own songs. For women to imitate men, or fail to make their own contribution, would be to defeat the purpose of their participation. This purpose is to assert and to emphasize the natural way of women in the scheme of life.

Women's authority over life and death extends to all matters affecting the security or continued life of the tribe. On this account some people even give women authority over the making of war. The Jabo tribe in Africa, for example, has two parliaments—the parliament of the young women and that of the older women. What these parliaments decide often becomes the law of the land. They decide that a stranger who wants to enter their country must not be admitted. And he is not admitted. They tell their men not to go to war and the men do not go.

To every people, war is both a religious undertaking and a practical task. Among primitive people it requires the services of women as the guardians of life. In their role of life givers they are indispensable to military victory. When the Haida Indian men go out to battle, the women sing and dance all night, pointing spears in the direction of the enemy. Women of the Karagive tribe accompany their men to war and beat the war drums. Scouting, fighting, inspiring men with courage, rejoicing at victory, lamenting the fallen, ensuring the continued life of their tribes, and performing different kinds of sympathetic magic with music are all activities regarded as normal for women in wartimes. (See Plate 4.)

Women's songs are valued as a means of transmitting strength to warriors. Among the Omaha Indians there is an old and untranslatable term, *We'Ton waan,* for those verses women sing in front of the empty tent of a man away at war:

> "The timid leader never wins fame,
> Let the tribes hear of you!" [11]

Through women the strength of the warrior may be preserved and transmitted to the tribe even in death. When an African Ibibio man is killed in battle, married women who are his next of kin rescue the corpse. No man may touch it. Weeping and singing sad songs, the scouts bear the dead warrior to a forest glade called *owokafai*— the place of those slain by sudden death. They lay him on a bed made of fresh leaves. Then they cut young branches from a sacred tree and wave the boughs over the genital organs of the warrior to extract his spirit of fertility into the leaves. Knowledge of the rites must be kept from men and from unmarried girls. Only married women, who have felt the virility of men in their bodies, can know the secret of life. To them it was entrusted by their great goddess "in the days when woman, not man, was the dominant sex . . . on the guarding of this secret depended the strength of the tribe. Were the rites once disclosed—few or no babes would be born, barns and herds would yield but scanty increase, while the arms of future generations of fighting men would lose their strength and hearts their courage." [12] This ceremony is conducted to the accompaniment of low, wailing chants, which only these wives of warriors have authority to sing, or even to know.

Even in places close to modern civilization the custom for choirs of women to sing the laments for warriors has persisted. On January 1, 1942, at Honolulu, when a funeral ceremony was held in memory of soldiers and sailors killed at Pearl Harbor, a choir of Polynesian women officiated. According to a newspaper account: "The silence was broken only by sobs and the soft chant for departed warriors sung by six native girls."

The association of women with war, and with music connected in various ways with war, is reflected in the fantastic figure of a terrible giantess. This Forest Demon of the Ibibios, whose women are so important in war and at the same time so musical, carries in her belly all the weapons in the world and also all the music. Bringing life to men engaged in a death struggle with the enemy and making appropriate music is thus impersonated by a woman spirit.

4.

The importance assigned to women in rites vital to the community stimulates women's musical talents. Because a woman is expected to give evidence of this life force flowing through her and because she has invented special powerful ways of using music for the benefit of her group, she is expected to make music. Primitive woman can be a successful musician because she is able both to realize and to idealize her natural capacities for work and for thought. Because her group demands music from her, she can assert and develop her native musical imagination.

Since women are expected to make important use of music, they have all the education in music the tribe can give them. Girls are trained in music and are given many opportunities for dancing, playing instruments, and singing. A girl lives her whole life among people who use music easily as a means of self-expression. She is as familiar with musical techniques as she is with speech and gestures. From the day she is born she hears the language of music and is taught to believe that it is a means of communication to be utilized at will. All children receive their first impressions of rhythm and melody from nurses, older sisters, mothers, and grandmothers. In many places, men initiates of religious cults learn the tribal songs and dances from the priestess in charge. Most primitive people regard women as peculiarly fitted by nature to think in terms of music; they consider music a direct extension of the functions of motherhood.

Talent and training in music are reinforced by adequate institutional support. Women's organization for making music is identical with their organization for the conduct of their worship, work, and play. The hierarchy of musicians consists of leaders, individual artists, and chorus. The chorus is the group of women who are performing their rites, working, or amusing themselves. The leaders and the professionals are the same women who have authority over the group in the ordinary course of daily life. The priestess-musician conducts the religious choir. The work leader conducts the singing of the women workers. In fact, a forewoman is often chosen for her ability to sing well and to have a large repertory of songs and stories. (See Plates 5 and 6.)

Both leaders and choir function under conditions that encourage them to do their best. Individual artists enjoy tremendous prestige and are often called in to perform at funerals, at weddings, and other occasions of community import. In North Russia, where the song leaders (*stihovóditzi*) are particularly musical, the chantress conducts the old rites and observes the old customs with authority often inherited through the mother's line. She knows by heart the ancient portions of the incantations and invocations that must be sung at every ceremony. She improvises new texts and new melodic lines to suit the emergency—a description of the virtues of the deceased, a history of the tribe, a portrayal of national characteristics, or whatever seems to be expected by her followers. The respect accorded her by both men and women is genuine, engendered by an inherited belief in her power to invoke the forces of life and by an admiration for her fertile imagination, which never fails to meet the artistic requirements of her group.

The women's choir functions at childbirth, at all rites of the rebirth, at work, at war, and for entertainment. According to local custom, the chorus sings in unison or in parts. In the Solomon Islands women sing thirds and fifths. In Papago Indian music a drone tone is held by women above the melody. Hottentot women often add a motif that, after an interval, they repeat with variations. An interesting type of part singing is performed by Russian singers. They develop variants to the melody, the effect being a rich harmonic structure quite different from the canonic imitation of western European polyphony. The responsorial form, in which the leader gives the first line of the verse and the chorus responds with additional lines, is universal. Antiphonal singing, which means that one group answers another group, is especially common among the Lithuanians, who, like many peasants, retain early customs. Among primitive women and many European peasant women the woman's chorus is as important a medium for the realization of women's musical ideas as is the solo singer. The solo singer's function is that of leader of the chorus. Though she may sing a portion of the song alone, she is primarily the spokeswoman for the group, who come in, rich and strong, with their own voices. The object of such singing is not the featuring of an individual, but collective expression under leadership.

Where women are recognized as having authority to make music for important ends, where training, organization, and incentives adequate for the kind of music expected of them are provided, primitive and peasant women living today are functioning as authoritative, creative musicians. No man makes their music for them; they make their own. No man leads them; they provide their own leaders. In their societies there is women's music—music conceived by women to fit their own experiences and to accompany their own activities. Women have their own dance steps, their own rhythmic patterns, and their own melodic lines. These are not, in any sense, imitative of men's, but spring wholly from the depths of their own approach to life and from associations lying deep in their inner lives. The explanation women themselves give of the nature of their songs is that some honored heroine or ancestress bequeathed the music to them, or else that they conceived it in a dream.

Though women imitate in their songs the natural sounds of the world around them, a man's voice is one natural sound that they do not imitate. In the entire range of the societies where women are creative musicians, instances of women assuming men's attitudes, taking over men's rites, singing in forced chest tones are rare and inconspicuous. On the other hand, instances of men wearing women's clothes, even castrating themselves, and singing in falsetto like women are, throughout history, frequent in men's religious ceremonies.

A complete collection of women's songs would fill many volumes, since, indeed, half of the folk songs and art songs of primitive and peasant people have been created by women, half of the total number of human beings. But our system of notation is, unfortunately, inadequate to reproduce them. On that account, many melodies to extant texts have been lost, or have become integrated into an ever changing musical idiom.

Wonderful songs and dances do not, of course, spring from every group of primitive people. Some races are not musically minded but develop their talents in other directions. Some merely make a noise with instruments and voice. But when a race is inclined to music, women as well as men, girls as well as boys evince the ability to think in terms of melody and rhythm, and even in harmony. It should be understood without laboring the point that women musicians of primitive and peasant societies are not to be compared to Bach, Beethoven, Brahms, and other musical giants of our civilization. These belong to an entirely different cultural level and cultural ideal. Primitive men are not creating harmony and counterpoint any more than are the women. But the music that women do create is of a quality and type entirely satisfactory to them and to their men, and is the highest that their culture knows. It requires for its composition, moreover, the same germ of emotional and artistic potency—the same capacity for symbolic thinking—that is required for the development of musical imagination at any time.

Most observers and historians of social activities in primitive tribes agree that the great school of primitive music owes its continuance to the woman musician. In both the quantity and the quality of music, women excel. Women dance more and sing more than men do. Women are the chief repositories for racial musical expression. It is they who store the incantations, the dirges, and the epics in their memories and who know the tribal lore. Women are also the chief transmitters of history, which is generally retailed in song and story. In the absence of written records, primitive music is passed on orally and often through the filter of woman's preconceived musical ideas, especially through lullabies and songs at initiation ceremonies.

Examples of primitive tribes in which women's musical activity is conspicuous in tribal life can be chosen from all types of humanity. Beginning in the north, the women of Kamchatka, of other aboriginal Siberian tribes, of the Eskimo peoples, especially those of Greenland, are outstanding musicians as compared to the men of their groups. In the Pacific islands, the Dyak women in Borneo excel in the music of their culture. The Trobriand Islanders, the Fiji Islanders, and many of the Maoris belong in this category. Among the black people of Africa the woman musician is in her element. Bushwomen, Pygmies, the Bavenda, the Ba-Ronga, the Valenge, Dahomeans, Ashantis, Wanyamwezi, the Tuareg, and many others represent woman's musical imagination in action.

Collectors of Oriental songs have commented on the extent of women's musical activity. In Tibet, for instance, and among the Dravidians of India, women musicians are outstanding. Grierson, who collected songs from different sets of people in India, said that

he could not have performed his task successfully if he had not had
access to the Hindu ladies' private quarters—the place where the
old songs were remembered and sung. Women in Siam and Cam-
bodia also excel as musicians. And Jewish women, wherever they
live, have a native talent for musical expression. (See Plate 18.)

In the group of European peasants, women musicians stand out
with undeniable power. Safarik, a prominent Slav scholar, said:
"Wherever there is a Slavonic woman, there also is a song." A good
half of the beautiful Russian, Yugoslavian, Bulgarian, Serbian, and
Albanian folk songs are the product of women's imagination—their
authorship in Russia being established by the use of verbs with feminine endings, such as *hodíla, trepála.* Fauriel, who collected Romaic
folk songs, commented upon the fact that many of the most beautiful were women's songs. The folk literature of Greece, Finland, Brit-
tany, Ireland, the Hebrides, and many other places is filled with
women's musical poems. Latvian, Estonian, and Lithuanian songs
are created almost entirely by women. In the vocal music of these
countries men play an altogether secondary role. In Lithuania, especially, the bulk of the musical literature consists of the women's ex-
quisite lyrics—the *daina.*

The manner of many European peasant women's singing is musicianship itself. The singers often have absolute pitch and are able
to dispense entirely with instrumental accompaniment. Voices are
true, strong, rich, and low. In one Lithuanian folk song a poetess-
musician asserts herself with these proud words:

> What a sonorous voice I have!
> It is as if it flowed in gold.
> People from afar are listening.[13]

The group singing of both primitive and peasant women is completely satisfying to performers and listeners. Just as the women are
sure of their own worth and confident that their music has a signifi-
cance for the whole society, so do their rich, warm voices require no
support from men or from instruments. The sounds produced by
peasant women in chorus are extravagantly admired by both musically untrained listeners and musicologists.

Music created by these peasant musicians is marked by great
vigor and richness of imagery, by highly ingenious rhythmic patterns, by a sensitivity to natural surroundings, by conspicuous

rites. It is true in the resurgent Indian movement of Latin Amer-
, in Mexico and Peru, and it is true in many parts of Russia. In
ese movements, which are political and social and only inciden-
lly artistic, there is usually a vigorous assertion of the values of that
pe of communal living in which women's talents as musicians and
ganizers of rites flowered.

It is true that the woman in these societies is not always a happy
eature, that she often lacks freedoms her civilized sisters enjoy,
nd that she submits to customs discriminatory to her sex. Neverthe-
ess, woman's authority as bearer of life is incorporated into religious
logma. Every individual woman in the tribe has an inestimable
piritual advantage. One of her great advantages is the assumption
hat the supreme life force may be feminine and manifested by
women. She is not limited to one male divinity with no feminine
religious officials.

In these lands where women make songs and folk tales set to
music, whatever a woman does, what she is, and what she is valued
for become projected into some kind of image or symbol. An outstanding woman becomes magnified and glorified into a goddess.
When Queen Oya of the Yoruba died about two hundred years ago
she was elevated to the rank of a divine power. Today homage is
paid to her as the spirit of the giant river Niger.

Hardly a primitive or peasant society exists without its spirits who
lead, protect, and represent women. For the Ibibios, the mother of
the town is a huge tree. Generation after generation of little brown
girls is presented to it. Often the guardian of women is a great rock
or water spirit. Often it is the moon. Again it is a supernatural
woman. Dzogbemesi—Woman of the Other World—receives the
prayers of the African Matse mothers. She punishes all those who
would harm her protégées, even their husbands. The Lithuanian
Mahra, with loosened hair streaming on her shoulders, holds a
woman in labor on her lap. Láda, in Russia, brings the flowers and
fruits of summer. "Mother" and "love" are the same word in the language of the Ibibios. Over them there rules a great life giver, whose
face is the face of love. This mother-love goddess—Eka Abassi—is
such an overwhelming power that no man dares approach her or
speak her name above a whisper.

Of all the symbols of womanhood, the moon is the most significant. The mysterious apparent synchronization of woman's monthly

beauty of melodic content, and by the same refine
that graced the art of the ancient Greek poetess-mu

The greatest heights of primitive and peasant musi
connection with those activities in which women hav
description, no recording, no evaluation of it can be m
without a recognition of the woman musician.

5.

It is easy for those who live within our own culture p
get how large a portion of the human race is outside thi
It is also easy to take no notice of the fact that, as peoples
pattern of western European civilization that was dom
World War II bestir and assert themselves, they are not
accepting the patterns that have prevailed in civilization
time.

All over the world there are still men and women who I
religion in which woman is the natural high priestess and
music. Many of these people are not to be regarded as u
remnants of old races who will ultimately be swept into the
of our present culture. On the contrary, most of them have
touch with our civilization for centuries, and are now unde
ministration of some government that offers them all modern
—British, French, Dutch, Russian, or American. Most of tl
nominally Christian, or are being actively proselytized by 1
aries. They have educated leaders trained in the best univers
Europe or America. Withal, in really vital matters they keep
nature religion and observe more or less the ancient festiv
which birth is the central mystery and woman the high priestes
by incantation or music to bend the unseen to her will.

One cannot see this nature religion anywhere in its entirety.
must put it together like the pieces of a picture puzzle—taki
birth rite from Africa, a puberty rite from central Asia—until
whole emerges. On the other hand, secret and unknown to 1
travelers as these customs are, incomplete, often quite archaic,
cannot underestimate their vitality. In the revolutionary ferment
over the world today, Christians with their roots in the woman's r
gion but with modern education are lustily reasserting themselv
This is true of the Maoris of New Zealand, whose Princess Te Puea
a genuine political force and earnestly calls for the maintenance (

beauty of melodic content, and by the same refined lyrical quality that graced the art of the ancient Greek poetess-musician.

The greatest heights of primitive and peasant music are reached in connection with those activities in which women have authority. No description, no recording, no evaluation of it can be made, therefore, without a recognition of the woman musician.

5.

It is easy for those who live within our own culture pattern to forget how large a portion of the human race is outside this way of life. It is also easy to take no notice of the fact that, as peoples outside the pattern of western European civilization that was dominant up to World War II bestir and assert themselves, they are not necessarily accepting the patterns that have prevailed in civilization up to this time.

All over the world there are still men and women who hold to the religion in which woman is the natural high priestess and maker of music. Many of these people are not to be regarded as uncivilized remnants of old races who will ultimately be swept into the currents of our present culture. On the contrary, most of them have been in touch with our civilization for centuries, and are now under the administration of some government that offers them all modern benefits —British, French, Dutch, Russian, or American. Most of them are nominally Christian, or are being actively proselytized by missionaries. They have educated leaders trained in the best universities of Europe or America. Withal, in really vital matters they keep to the nature religion and observe more or less the ancient festivals, of which birth is the central mystery and woman the high priestess, able by incantation or music to bend the unseen to her will.

One cannot see this nature religion anywhere in its entirety. One must put it together like the pieces of a picture puzzle—taking a birth rite from Africa, a puberty rite from central Asia—until the whole emerges. On the other hand, secret and unknown to most travelers as these customs are, incomplete, often quite archaic, one cannot underestimate their vitality. In the revolutionary ferment all over the world today, Christians with their roots in the woman's religion but with modern education are lustily reasserting themselves. This is true of the Maoris of New Zealand, whose Princess Te Puea is a genuine political force and earnestly calls for the maintenance of the rites. It is true in the resurgent Indian movement of Latin America, in Mexico and Peru, and it is true in many parts of Russia. In these movements, which are political and social and only incidentally artistic, there is usually a vigorous assertion of the values of that type of communal living in which women's talents as musicians and organizers of rites flowered.

It is true that the woman in these societies is not always a happy creature, that she often lacks freedoms her civilized sisters enjoy, and that she submits to customs discriminatory to her sex. Nevertheless, woman's authority as bearer of life is incorporated into religious dogma. Every individual woman in the tribe has an inestimable spiritual advantage. One of her great advantages is the assumption that the supreme life force may be feminine and manifested by women. She is not limited to one male divinity with no feminine religious officials.

In these lands where women make songs and folk tales set to music, whatever a woman does, what she is, and what she is valued for become projected into some kind of image or symbol. An outstanding woman becomes magnified and glorified into a goddess. When Queen Oya of the Yoruba died about two hundred years ago she was elevated to the rank of a divine power. Today homage is paid to her as the spirit of the giant river Niger.

Hardly a primitive or peasant society exists without its spirits who lead, protect, and represent women. For the Ibibios, the mother of the town is a huge tree. Generation after generation of little brown girls is presented to it. Often the guardian of women is a great rock or water spirit. Often it is the moon. Again it is a supernatural woman. Dzogbemesi—Woman of the Other World—receives the prayers of the African Matse mothers. She punishes all those who would harm her protégées, even their husbands. The Lithuanian Mahra, with loosened hair streaming on her shoulders, holds a woman in labor on her lap. Láda, in Russia, brings the flowers and fruits of summer. "Mother" and "love" are the same word in the language of the Ibibios. Over them there rules a great life giver, whose face is the face of love. This mother-love goddess—Eka Abassi—is such an overwhelming power that no man dares approach her or speak her name above a whisper.

Of all the symbols of womanhood, the moon is the most significant. The mysterious apparent synchronization of woman's monthly